Introduc

The Brecon Beacons National Park stretches
Carmarthenshire, a distance of nearly 50 miles, cover
southern Wales is divided into four distinct areas of high
rivers, here in their enthusiastic infancy, descend to meet
three great cities of the south, Newport, Cardiff and Swansea respectively.

Strictly speaking the term 'Brecon Beacons' applies to the central area of the Park, just south of Brecon. In particular, to the three or four highest peaks, crowned by Pen y Fan. At 886 metres its distinctive cap is the highest land in southern Britain and only just fails to break through the magic 3000 feet mark. These sandstone peaks are buttressed by a series of high ridges nurturing the infant waters of the Taf to the south and tributaries of the Usk to the north. The phrase 'Central Beacons' is sometimes used to distinguish this area from the entire National Park that extends much further.

However, there are two further mountain blocks westwards from here. These are more remote and relatively undiscovered. To the west is Fforest Fawr, a wild expanse of upland that stretches from the A470 to the pass between the headwaters of the Tawe and Usk.

Beyond this, to the far west, the Black Mountain covers a vast expanse of remote and lonely moorland beyond the sources of the Tawe and Usk. It rises to a remarkable serrated edge that stretches for over five miles, known as the 'Carmarthen Fan'.

This guidebook covers these central and western areas of the National Park. Another Kittiwake guide, 'Walking in the Black Mountains', covers the eastern mountain range. These summits and high moorland cocoon a sequence of wooded valleys as far as the final ridge on the English border.

The Central Beacons, Fforest Fawr and the Black Mountain share geological features. The northern moors and escarpments expose red sandstone. In the Beacons, this culminates in the distinctive sloping plateaux on the summits of Corn Du and Pen y fan, presiding over the Usk valley and hills of mid Wales beyond (Walks 15-18). In Fforest Fawr, the spectacular, hidden alpine cliffs of Craig Cerrig-gleisiad and Craig Cwm-du also look northwards (Walks 19-20). To the west, Walks 1 and 2 explore the extended and remote ridge of Carmarthen Fan. To the south, limestone comes to the surface and gives an entirely different character to the topography and fauna. These porous rocks gestate the young Taf Fechan and Nedd Fechan which, with their tributaries, have carved dramatic gorges and spectacular waterfalls (Walks 5-7). Swansea's river, the Tawe, also crosses limestone and its upper valley hides the biggest cave system in Wales (Walks 3 and 4). There are many other highlights to visit, including Wales' only distillery (Walk 6) and the impressive limestone quarries at Mynydd Llangatwg (Walk 14). A number of walks enjoy a section on the tranquil Brecon and Monmouthshire Canal (9, 14), follow forest trails (7) or discover a steam railway (10). A great starting point for new or regular visitors is the National Park's Mountain Centre just south of Brecon (Walk 20).

Walks in this book vary from 2 to over 10 miles. Many are serious mountain expeditions. Weather makes a huge difference to the seriousness of a walk in this upland region. Conditions change quickly so please take care and keep safe. Most of the walks are across remote or mountain terrain, though some are more moderate and offer shorter alternatives. Take mountain precautions, taking extra food, drinks, spare clothing and waterproofs. Carry a first aid kit and an emergency 'bivvy' bag. Take and use a large-scale map to supplement the plans in this book. OS Explorer 12 and 13 cover all the walks. Wear boots and be prepared to use a compass or GPS equipment. Tell someone where you are going and stick to your route. *Never be too proud to turn back.* Remember, the mountains will still be here tomorrow.

If you want some gentler adventures, another book, 'Short Walks in the Brecon Beacons' offers a range of 20 shorter 'mini-expeditions' across the whole National Park.

This is a wonderful area to walk, with a huge variety of scenery and much of interest. Enjoy it!

BANNAU SIR GAER & LLYN Y FAN FACH

DESCRIPTION An expedition on to the dramatic ridge of Bannau Sir Gaer, or Carmarthen Fan. An alluring track ventures into the remote and legendary cwm of Llyn y Fan Fach. The walk then climbs onto the ridge and around the craggy edge of the impressive cirque. There are spectacular views, but TAKE CARE!

DISTANCE & TERRAIN 6 miles there and back to Picws Du; 7½ to Fan Foel. Excellent track to Llyn y Fan Foel, then clear but exposed mountain paths. Some steady climbing. Return route includes an (avoidable) river crossing.

START Parking area near Llanddeusant, SN 797238. Llanddeusant lies just off the minor road from Trecastle. From Llanddeusant, follow the signs to Llyn y Fan along a narrow lane. When the surfaced road ends, continue along the track for a further mile until it ends at a parking area just past a farm. You can't drive any further along the track after this point.

I *The car park is a wonderful spot in itself, so linger a moment to enjoy the tranquillity and drama of the head of the valley, presided over by the great wall of Bannau Sir Gaer. The remoteness is tangible, with bracken, gorse and loose rock clothing the rising hillsides. Small streams drain the waterlogged slopes and coalesce to the stream at the bottom of the valley, feeding the young Afon Sawdde.* Follow the track which gradually ascends alongside its tumbling headwaters, making directly for the mountain ridge above. After ½ mile, pass a trout hatchery and continue on the track, heading resolutely for the dramatic cirque of mountains enclosing the glacial cwm of Llyn y Fan Fach. About 1½ mile after the start, arrive at the lake, contained by a small dam, and accompanied by an old building, useful as a shelter. *The lake is over 1600 feet above sea level and ensconced in an enchanting hanging valley, encircled by cliffs.*

2 Just in front of the old building, where the track bends to the left around the dam, leave it and take a mountain path to the right. This makes a relatively easy ascent up the grassy slopes to the right of the forbidding great wall of crags. The climb is steady but moderate and later becomes an engineered stony path, curving round to the edge of the ridge. As you reach the ridge, notice a grass path sidling in from the right; this is the Beacons Way long distance path. The junction is not very distinct but it's worth noting now as the turning point for the return route.

3 For now, continue ahead on the path around the edge of the ridge. *The view across the cwm is truly breath-taking; the precipice is to be admired but treated with great respect, especially in wind or ice! The route hugs the edge of the ridge with views west now across the contrasting pastoral landscape of Carmarthenshire.* Level off on to a grass plateau, crowned by a cairn, at 2200 feet above sea level. *Having gained the ridge, there are extensive views south, miles of wilderness and open moorland stretching down towards the Swansea Valley and, in the distance, the Gower peninsula.* The path continues near the edge of the vertical abyss, rounding the corner of the cirque at the head of a deeply eroded gulley and then heading directly towards Picws Du. The route undulates along the edge and then a moderate climb up a grassy slope leads to the summit at 2457 feet.

4 From Picws Du a clear path continues to Fan Foel. It descends steeply to Bwlch Blaen-Twrch and then rises up the opposite slopes to the flat, pointed plateau of Fan Foel, protruding northwards from the main ridge like the bow of a ship. The terrain here is bare and quite confusing. There are paths across the 'prow' but you can also follow the path near the edge of the escarpment to reach a cairn with a large circular base at the head of the plateau.

5 You can continue on to Bannau Brycheiniog if you wish (see walk 2) or even tramp on to Glyntawe in the Swansea ground, slightly below the crest of the ridge. *Enjoy views across the cwm and the lake.* Eventually, it curves round the crest of the ridge and descends the broad grass shoulder of Cefn Nant Lygos. Approaching the bottom, cross a marshy area. The Beacons Way goes straight on to a gate at the bottom left hand corner and descends through woodland to reach the valley road. Alternatively, pick up a track slanting down to the right which reaches the stream close to the car park. The only drawback of this direct route is the need to ford the stream, best done almost opposite the parking area. When the river is in spate this may be challenging, but the alternative Beacons Way route can be used instead.

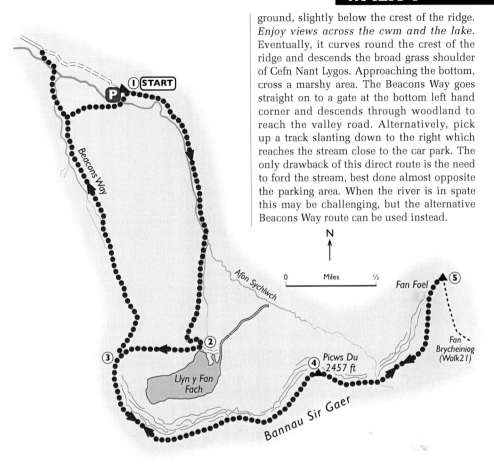

valley, though for the latter option you would need to make arrangements for a lift back!

To return to the start, retrace your steps along the ridge as far as Point 3. Although there are alternative routes, these use steep paths down the escarpment and difficult, boggy routes around the base. These routes cannot compare to the excellent ridge and it is worth sampling the views in the return direction.

From Point 3, leave the main path where it gently swerves to the right, leaving the highest ground to descend to Llyn y Fan Fach. The junction isn't that clear, and the path is a grassy sheep track. It is more easily spotted ahead of the bifurcation, so if visibility is good, pinpoint it in advance. The path, the Beacons Way, continues along the high

The Lady of the Lake
Unsurprisingly, the lake is the venue for an ancient and tragic legend, the Lady of the Lake. After many attempts at courting, a local young man was allowed to marry the beautiful and mysterious lady of the lake, endowed by as many animals as she could count in one breath. There was a condition: he would not strike her three times. A series of events led to a sequence of three strikes, such as tapping her on the shoulder to stop her laughing during a funeral. She returned to the lake, taking all the animals with her. Their three sons searched for her and became doctors, the renowned Physicians of Myddfai.

FAN BRYCHEINIOG

DESCRIPTION A 5 mile escarpment extends around the eastern and northern edge of the Black Mountain, producing an eye catching profile to the north and offering a sustained high level walk around the edge of the remote wilderness. Collectively the whole ridge is often referred to as Carmarthen Fan, but it is in two sections. The north facing crag, Bannau Sir Gaer (Carmarthenshire Beacon), forms a dramatic cliff cirque around Llyn y Fan Fach and continues east as far as Fan Foel. Its highest point is Picws Du. From Fan Foel, the east facing scarp, Bannau Brycheiniog), cradles Llyn y Fan Fawr and reaches its highest point at Fan Brycheiniog. This is the highest point in the western Beacons at 2631 feet. There are far fewer paths and passable routes across this western area of the national park and the ridge also offers a relatively easy promenade with unparalleled views.

This walk climbs the ridge from the south, reaching the tops from Glyntawe, an idyllic spot in the upper Swansea Valley. The walk is 'twinned' with Walk 1 which approaches Carmarthen Fan from the north.

DISTANCE & TERRAIN 8 miles out and back. A long ascent and a ridge walk. Remote country with steep edges, requiring care at all times, but especially in windy or icy conditions. The route is generally clear but navigational skill and a compass are required in mist, especially around Fan Foel.

START Tafarn-y-Garreg pub, Glyntawe. Use the roadside lay-by close by. SN 848172. Glyntawe is in the upper Swansea valley on the main A4067 Swansea-Brecon road. Bus service 63 Swansea-Ystradgynlais-Brecon.

I The footpath starts opposite the pub and is signed as the Beacons Way. Cross a footbridge over the River Tawe and walk alongside the river for about 300 yards before turning left through a gate. Climb towards some sheep pens, passing to the right of them and then cross a stile on to the open mountain side. Although not marked on the OS map, there is a clear path which climbs steeply and directly up the hillside, through bracken and stones. After about ½ mile it levels out and passes round the knoll of Allt Fach. Cross a small, soggy depression before climbing again, this time more gently. There is a long and steady ascent up the moorland slope of Fan Hir, now clearly seen ahead. Although the route is generally clear, it's worth clocking your route for the return journey as there are one or two ambiguous twists and turns. *As you gain height, look eastwards over the shapely profile of Fan Gyhirych to the twin sandstone peaks of the Beacons, Pen y Fan and Corn Du. There are also panoramic views down the Swansea valley.* About 2 miles after the start of the walk, you reach the edge of the steep escarpment and begin the long ridge of Carmarthen Fan, which snakes for over four miles above the twin lakes of Llyn y Fan Fawr and Llyn y Fan Fach. The first stage is the long traverse of Fan Hir (in Welsh, 'the long beacon'). The precipice drops abruptly to the squelchy grasslands below. Walk along the edge, climbing steadily with sandstone rocks replacing the ubiquitous grass until you reach the northern and highest end of Fan Hir, a whisker under 2500 feet above sea level and nearly 2000 feet above Glyntawe.

2 From the summit of Fan Hir, the path drops down to Bwlch Giedd. A steep path brings the low level route of the Beacons Way up from the shores of Llyn y Fan Fawr. Climb the stepped path to conquer the summit of Fan Brycheiniog (The Breconshire Beacon). This is the highest point on the whole ridge at 2631 feet. There is a trig point and circular shelter here to mark the top. *It is worth spending some time here to savour the wide views: eastwards across the Beacons to the Black Mountains; southwards across South Wales and the Bristol Channel as far as Somerset and Devon on a clear day!*

3 Beyond the trig point, the path curves round to the north cairn. It then veers left, remaining on the edge of the mountain, reaching Fan Foel about ¼ mile later. The circular base of a cairn adorns the plateau.

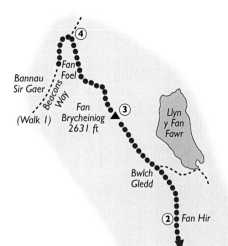

4 At Fan Foel, the ridge protrudes northwards like the prow of a ship. From here look out across the hills and moors of Mid Wales. *This is also a historic site and remains of flints and clay beads have been found around the remains of the cairn here.* Return to Glyntawe by the same route, or, if you want a longer adventure, descend the side of Fan Foel to Bwlch Blaen Twrch before climbing steeply to the summit of Bannau Sir Gaer (see Walk 1).

If you have arranged a lift, you can continue along the whole ridge before descending to the dam of Llyn y Fan Fach and following the reservoir track down towards Llanddeusant.

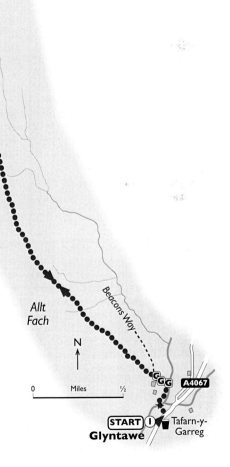

CRIBARTH

DESCRIPTION A layer of limestone is exposed along the southern edge of the National Park. This has produced natural wonders like the waterfalls of Pontneddfechan or the caves of Dan-yr-Ogof. In places it has also been exploited for industrial use through quarrying and lime production, though the historic remains only enhance the majesty and fascination of the untamed mountains. Cribarth is one such example. Its jagged profile stands guard over the Swansea valley above Abercraf. Its resources have been hewed and its wilderness crossed by tramways, but its open limestone heights offer peaceful heathland and splendid views.

DISTANCE & TERRAIN 5 miles. Steep climb then mountain and heathland paths, rough in places. Beware of old workings around the higher parts of Cribarth.

START Craig-y-nos Country Park SN 840155. Craig-y-nos lies in the upper Swansea valley, just south of Glyntawe on the A4067 Swansea – Brecon road. Bus 63 (Brecon-Ystradgynlais-Swansea) serves the main road. There is a National Park Visitor Centre here, with a café and pay and display parking, contributing to the National Park's work of conservation and recreation. Other local attractions include the Dan-yr-Ogof show caves and the Shire Horse Centre, as well as the country park itself.

I From the entrance to the car park, turn left and walk along the side of the main road for about 300 yards. Then cross a stile on the opposite side of the road, bearing right along a track signed, 'The open hill and geological trail'. Follow this for about 100 yards until you come to a barrier. In front of this double back to the right, climbing steeply on a clear path through limestone and rough heath land. Higher up the path climbs around the knoll to a wall and stile. Cross this into open grassland.

2 From the stile, bear right, following the wall for a few yards but then, as the wall drops away to the right, maintain the line to gain the main ridge of Cribarth. There are lots of different paths and tracks on the open limestone heathland, studded with outcrops and loose stones. Which track you follow along the top is of little consequence, always taking care of former workings and natural hazards. Keep to the left of some old quarry workings and then pick up a clearer path. Later you will notice a depression, including the line of a tramway which ran across the edge of the quarries just below the crest of the ridge. Continue through the depression, later accompanied by a wall on the left. The crags of Cribarth now rise up to the right. Although the direct route continues along the depression, you will want to make the short climb to the summit, marked by a shiny white trig point. *Enjoy the views south along the Swansea valley to Ystradgynlais or north to the shapely peak of Fan Gyhirych.* Return from the summit to the wall and depression. The path weaves downhill alongside the wall, then passes some old workings at the bottom. As the limestone gives way to marshy and rougher terrain, look out for a wooden stile in the stone wall to the left.

3 Cross this and bear left to follow a footpath around the hillside. The tussocks give way to bilberries and then heather as you descend to the top of an incline, arriving at a fence and stile. Don't cross this. Instead, in front of it, turn left, following the path towards Ynyswen. The path weaves its way down the rough hillside, with stones and bracken abounding. *The village below in the valley is Abercraf.* A final marshy section, tamed by duckboards, leads to a stile. Turn left and walk along the bottom edge of three fields, just above woodland. Then cross back onto the open hillside. The path meanders, but essentially contours the side of Cribarth, its serrated edge piercing the skyline. *Look ahead to the pyramid of Fan Gyhirych, its lower slopes smothered with conifer plantations.* Continue for about ½ mile. When you come to a wall, the path turns directly downhill to meet a gate in the corner of the field, next to a house.

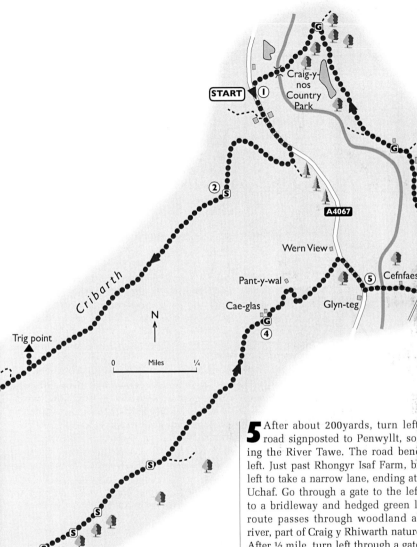

5 After about 200 yards, turn left along a road signposted to Penwyllt, soon crossing the River Tawe. The road bends to the left. Just past Rhongyr Isaf Farm, branch off left to take a narrow lane, ending at Rhongyr Uchaf. Go through a gate to the left leading to a bridleway and hedged green lane. The route passes through woodland above the river, part of Craig y Rhiwarth nature reserve. After ½ mile, turn left through a gate into the Craig y Nos Country Park and back to the start.

Craig-y-nos Country Park

Craig-y-nos first developed as an estate in the mid nineteenth century. The house was used as a hospital between 1919 and 1980, but in 1976 the Brecon Beacons National Park Authority turned the grounds into a country park. There are woods, riverside walks and meadows to enjoy and a Visitor Centre interprets the landscape.

4 Pass through the gate below the house and a further one onto a lane. Follow this downhill. At the bottom reach the main road and turn right. Take care here, as there is no pavement.

WALK 4

GLYNTAWE & PENWYLLT

DESCRIPTION This walk is short in distance, but rich in historical and geological interest. During the course of 4 miles you encounter the remains of one of the highest railways in Wales, while under your feet lies the deepest cave system in the country. In between, the infant River Tawe forges a path through spectacular limestone crags and the attractive arbour of Craig-y-nos Country Park.

DISTANCE & TERRAIN 4 miles. Quite an intricate route through country park, nature reserve and limestone heath.

START Craig-y-nos Country Park. SN 840155. Craig-y-nos lies aside the A4067 Swansea – Brecon road in the upper Swansea valley, just south of Glyntawe. There is a National Park Visitor Centre here. The car park charge contributes to the National Park's work of conservation and recreation, so pay it with a good heart! Bus 63 Brecon-Ystradgynlais-Swansea serves the main road.

1 Start outside the Visitor Centre and go down the steps in front of you. Follow the path through a brick gateway, past the fishpond and down to the river. Turn right, passing a confluence of rivers and then turn left to cross the Afon Tawe by a footbridge. On the far side turn left to follow the Tawe upstream.

2 In about a quarter of a mile, some stepping-stones lead across the river. This would be an unwise choice and risky enterprise! Instead, cross the convenient footbridge and go through a gate. Cross a small but rather soggy wood to another gate. Beyond this follow the way marks through a marshy area, helped by duckboards. Cross a stile to reach the main road. Cross carefully and reach a stile on the opposite side. Follow the path between two fields and climb slightly to reach a car park. Turn right through the car park. *As you are about to pass the wide access road, notice a recon-structed dolmen on your right, interpreting a prehistoric burial site. The stone circles only date from the year 2000, erected to celebrate the present millennium!* Keep ahead past the access road, towards the campsite. *On your right is the Shire Horse Centre. The field may also be home to other animals including goats, sheep and llamas.*

3 At the end of the animal field, turn left, following a finger post off the road. The path now climbs left above the campsite. After a kissing gate, pass a sheepfold and keep straight ahead as the path descends to the rocky bed of the Afon Haffes. Cross the water at a convenient place, making use of the stones. This is not especially hazardous in normal conditions, but care is needed on the rocks and especially if they are slippery or the river is in spate. On the opposite bank, look for a gate and stile in the fence. Follow the path and lane down through a series of gates and past a restored house until you reach the main road.

4 Cross the road and follow it left for a short distance, crossing the River Tawe. Opposite a phone box, turn right along Heol Callwen. Continue past the houses and on to Pwllcoediog Farm. In the farmyard, turn left following a public footpath sign. Climb diagonally up the hillside crossing a series of stiles. After a patch of woodland you soon emerge at the top. *A completely different landscape lies ahead of you and the bustle of the valley is left behind. In front lies a lunar terrain of limestone crags, pockmarked by quarries and loose rocks.* Follow the path as it weaves a way past a disused quarry and emerges on to a lane. You have now reached the old quarrying village of Penwyllt. Turn left and follow the lane a short way to its terminus.

5 In front of you are the remains of Penwyllt railway station, complete with platforms and station buildings. Beyond lies Penwyllt quarry. Turn right past the station and follow the stony road round the perimeter of the quarry. This ends at a row of old quarry houses, now a caving centre. Just before this a footpath sign indicates the cross-country route to the Nedd Fechan valley. A bleak but atmospheric cross country route now followed by the Beacons Way leads east to join Sarn Helen, the old Roman road, about 3½ miles to the south east. Turn right and follow the path through a kissing gate and across the track of the old railway. Negotiate the accompanying ditch, cross a stile and follow the path up to a ruined building, noting remains of lime kilns to the left. Just in front of the house turn right and follow the track across the rough pasture. It returns to the top of the road, just near the station at point 5. Turn left and follow the road downhill.

6 About 100 yards after a bungalow on your right, where the road begins to veer to the left, go through a gate on the right hand side, indicated by a bridle way sign. Descend the valley amidst bracken and flowers. Towards the bottom it becomes more wooded and stony. At the end, go through a gate and turn right on to the tarmac lane. Follow this a few yards to its end in front of Rhongyr-uchaf farm. A gate just to the left of the house gives access to a walled lane through the woods. In just over half a mile, turn left through a gate in the fence on your left. Follow the path for a few yards back to point 2 by the stepping-stones. Turn left and retrace your steps back to the Visitor Centre.

Dan-yr-ogof

You can explore part of the vast labyrinth of limestone caverns at Dan-yr-ogof, where the River Llynell emerges from the rock. Among other attractions on the site are the Shire Horse Centre, a dinosaur park, and a reconstruction of a 100-year old farm. (Entrance charge).

Penwyllt

High on a shelf above the Tawe valley, Penwyllt developed as a centre for limestone quarrying and the production of lime. Silica sand was also extracted nearby. Between 1867 and 1962 passenger trains ran between Neath and Brecon. The station at Penwyllt, still broadly intact, was paid for by Adelina Platt, the opera singer, who lived at Craig-y-nos. Ogof Ffynnon Ddu Nature reserve extends from Penwyllt across a large area of limestone crag and pavement beyond. In English the name translates as 'cave of the black spring', the deepest cave system in Britain.

PONT MELIN FACH & WATERFALL COUNTRY

DESCRIPTION The Mellte, Hepste and Nedd Fechan all drain the wild limestone uplands in the southern part of the national park. As they travel south, they cross belts of harder sandstone rock, which the water has eroded less than the neighbouring shale. Here is where the waterfalls are formed. This is a popular area of the national park, often referred to as 'Waterfall Country'. There is a range of walks for all abilities. Paths pass through wooded gorges where fast flowing streams tumble down spectacular waterfalls on their way from the mountains to the sea.

DISTANCE & TERRAIN 6 miles. The first section follows the Nedd Fechan from Pontneddfechan to Pont Melin Fach known as the 'Elidir Trail'. The fast flowing river travels down a series of falls, viewed from the path. After Pont Melin Fach, a quiet lane climbs to common land at Comin y Rhos, with extensive views across the forest away to the sea beyond. A woodland track descends to the opposite bank of the Nedd Fechan for the final leg. Shorter linear alternatives are described below.

START Opposite the Angel Hotel, Pontneddfechan. SN 902076. There are toliets, a small car park and some roadside parking here. Bus service from Neath to Pontneddfechan. The village of Pontneddfechan lies close to the A465 Hirwaun-Neath road. Leave this main road at Glyn-neath and follow the signs.

I Pass through the iron gates marked 'Sgwd Gwladus'. Follow the path, which is suitable for pushchairs and wheelchairs for the first mile. *It follows the line of an old tramway and the stone setts are still visible in places. Mixed deciduous woodland, including sycamore, beech and oak trees, provide habitats for a variety of woodland birds. You may see grey wagtails or dippers in the river itself. There are some cave entrances in the rocks on the left.* A picnic area marks the limit of navigation for pushchairs and wheelchairs. The path continues up some steps and onwards to the confluence of the Nedd Fechan and Pyrddin at Pwll Du ar Byrddin.

2 From here you can visit Sgwd Gwladus by keeping left and following the path to the pretty waterfall. Return to the junction at point 2. Then cross the footbridge and pass a finger post. Keep to the left hand bank of the Nedd Fechan, ignoring the second footbridge and following the sign to Pont Melin Fach. The path clings to the side of the river, passing a series of waterfalls. *Ravines cut into the cliffs, gouged out by water cascading down into the river below.* The gorge opens out at the picnic area and car park at Pont Melin Fach.

3 Turn right and cross the road bridge. Follow the quiet lane as it twists uphill to the common at Comin y Rhos. *Magnificent views are your reward. The slightly raised ground offers unimpeded vistas of a wide segment of southern Wales. If the air is clear, look southwest to see the rocks of Mumbles reaching out into Swansea Bay.* Carry on past the crossroads on the top of the common. Where the open land ends, turn right across a cattle grid to follow the access road towards Gwernblaedde Farm. Continue past the farm and the water treatment works until the road becomes a forest track. This ends by a house at Glan-yr-afon. Follow the path left from here. It descends through woodland to meet the river at the bottom.

4 Turn left to follow the riverside path signed for Pontneddfechan. In places it is narrow and requires some care. At a finger post it doubles back and zigzags up the hill away from the river. At the top cross a stile and follow the path with the fence on your right through light woodland. Cross a footbridge guarded by two stiles. At the far side choose the left hand of two stiles and make your way through a short section of soggy woodland, past a school and on to the road. You are now in Pontneddfechan. Turn right down the road between the houses. At a bend, by a bus shelter, follow a lane straight ahead. This drops down, and ends at the top of some steps, which lead you back to the Angel Hotel and the start of the walk.

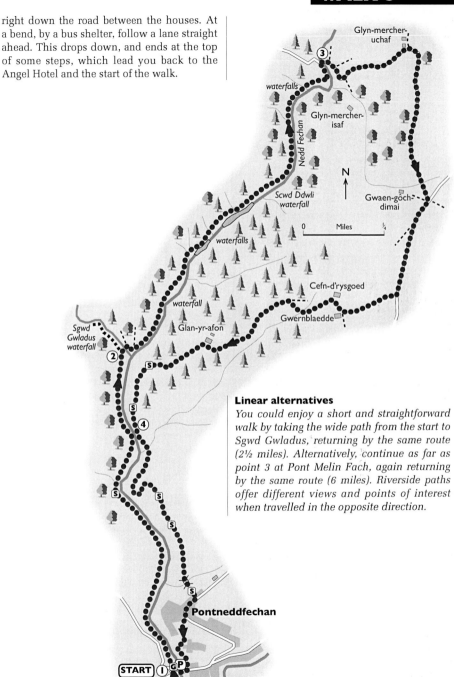

Linear alternatives

You could enjoy a short and straightforward walk by taking the wide path from the start to Sgwd Gwladus, returning by the same route (2½ miles). Alternatively, continue as far as point 3 at Pont Melin Fach, again returning by the same route (6 miles). Riverside paths offer different views and points of interest when travelled in the opposite direction.

WALK 6

WHISKEY & WATERFALLS

DESCRIPTION An interesting circuit of woods and uplands at the southern end of 'Waterfall Country'. The outward section climbs through attractive heath and moor to the village of Penderyn, home of Wales' only distillery. The return follows a wooded ridge high above the gorge carved by the Afon Mellte on its way through the limestone bedrock. The noise of birdsong and waterfalls accompany you much of the way.

DISTANCE & TERRAIN 5½ miles. Heath and woodland paths with moderate climbs. The route can be muddy between points 2 and 3. Please note the comments below about Sgwd yr Eira.

START Forestry Commission car park at Dinas Rock, Pontneddfechan SN 911079. Pontneddfechan sits astride the confluence of the Nedd Fechan and Mellte rivers at the foot of 'Waterfall Country'. To reach the village, leave the A465 Hirwaun-Neath road at Glyn-neath and follow the signs. To find the start of Walk 6 continue past the information centre for another half mile until you reach the end of the road and the Dinas Rock car park. Note that the car park is locked after dark

I Climb the stony track just to the north of the car park, signposted to the waterfalls. This rises up the side of the rock, Craig-y-ddinas, and on through the woods. It climbs along a narrow neck of limestone rock between the Afon Mellte and a small tributary. *Quarrying has eaten into the bedrock, but the crag is capped by delightful limestone heathland with soft, springy turf.* At the top of the heath, keep to the right alongside the fence. The path passes through an area of old quarries and rises up through the bracken. There is now a long, but steady ascent on a charming bridleway. *The views widen.* Beyond a gate you enter wilder country. *In the distance on the right, you can see the site of Tower Colliery, Wales' last deep coal mine, closed in 2008.* After the summit

the track descends gently towards Penderyn. It joins a small tarmac lane through a gate. Follow this ahead as it winds around St Cynog's church. *This has been a Christian place of worship since the sixth century and the graveyard is now maintained as a wild-life haven.* The lane drops down to skirt the village of Penderyn. Unless visiting the village continue straight ahead until the last houses. A diversion to the right will bring you to the main road, a pub and a bus stop. *Not far from here is Wales' only distillery, making Penderyn whiskey.*

2 Turn left along a track in front of a couple of cottages. A footpath sign set a little way back indicates the route to Sgwd yr Eira. At the end of the lane a gate leads into open access land. The track follows the course of an old tramway and soon comes to some old quarries. Keep beside the fence on your right and follow the guide marks, crossing an area of damp rough pasture towards some trees. Cross the stile and bear left up the side of the plantation. Soon the ground drops away towards the Hepste valley. The path goes through some soggy patches but the line is clear.

To Pontneddfechan

Craig-y-ddinas

(i) (P)

(START) Dinas Rock

3 Arrive at a finger post pointing the way down to Sgwd yr Eira, whose Welsh name means 'waterfall of the snow'. *You can hear the noise as a curtain of water plunges down a rocky cliff amidst dense woodland.* The path leads down to the fall itself, it is steep and can be tricky. If you venture down, be careful of wet rocks and you are advised by signs not to go behind the waterfall itself. *Nevertheless it is an impressive sound and sight to view the three curtains of water thundering over the rock face into the pool below.* Walk 7 visits Sgwd yr Eira from the opposite site, starting at Cwm Porth. Having viewed the falls, return back up to the steep climb to the finger post. From here, take the path towards Craig-y-ddinas. The route now follows the top of the limestone gorge. *Soon*

Sgwd yr Eira
waterfall

③

N

Cilhepste-fach

S

S

0   Miles   ½

A4059

G

Tor-y-foel ②

Penderyn

Moel Penderyn

G

G

G

G

G

Clwyd-rhyd-fan

Swansea. Continue on this path as it returns to the limestone heath and quarries at Craig-y-ddinas and descends to the car park and starting point.

Craig-y-ddinas

An old legend claims that Craig-y-ddinas is the rock under which King Arthur sleeps, waiting to rescue Wales from the Saxon invaders. A tale relates how a Welshman from London visited a cavern under the rock and found the king, with his knights, asleep inside. He was told he could take the gold and silver from the slumbering heroes, but had to remember to tell them to 'sleep on'. On the first occasion he remembered, but forgot on his second trip. His greed was met with destruction.

there are picturesque views across the forest, with the confluence of Mellte and Hepste rivers hidden in the trees below. Later you can see the Neath valley snaking its way towards

Sgwd yr Eira

THE FOUR FALLS TRAIL

DESCRIPTION Most of this walk is on a waymarked trail devised by the National Park Authority so it is easy to follow and explores some of the most interesting parts of the forested limestone area around the south of the Park. The Four Falls Trail is marked by red posts between Points 2 and 5 on the map.

DISTANCE & TERRAIN 4 miles plus detours to waterfalls. Forest tracks and paths, mostly excellent. However, the paths down to the water are steep and narrow, requiring due diligence.

START Cwm Porth car park (charge), situated on a minor road, off the road between Ystradfellte and Penderyn, SN 928124. There is an information cabin and shop here, as well as toilets. This is also a popular starting point for exploring nearby caves and limestone formations.

1 From the entrance to the car park cross the road and take the footpath signposted to Sgwd Clun-Gwyn. Pass the entrance to the caves, continuing on the main footpath along the left hand side of a limestone ravine, gouged out by water. *Loose boulders are encrusted with mosses and lichens.* The path soon drops down to the water's edge and then accompanies the river, with clumps of primroses adorning the opposite bank in season. *Fields give way to a rocky woodland path, with grey wagtails bobbing on stones in the water, and alder trees draping over the bank.* Some careful footwork is needed where gnarled tree roots have eroded the bank. The valley widens out into a grassy meadow as it approaches a footbridge. Stay on the left hand bank and climb some stone steps to a broader path. This now rises above the valley and comes to a junction. (There is a short steep path to the right down to Sgwd Llyn Gwyn. To view the first fall follow this down to the river and return to this point).

2 Join the Four Falls Trail here, following it in an anticlockwise direction. Bear right following the trail past post 16 to weave over a small gulley. Continue on the Trail past post 17 through limestone woodland, high above the gorge. Later cross a footbridge into conifer trees. Continue to ascend along the edge of the gorge. When you reach post 22, you realise the enormity of the limestone gorge and cliffs. You can't see Sgwd Isaf Clun-Gwyn below, but you can hear the water cascading over the fall. Continue on the Trail until signpost 25.

3 A steep rocky path leads sharply to the right downhill to Sgwd y Pannwr, about ⅓ mile away. Return to this point if you view the fall. The main track continues straight ahead towards Sgwd y Eira on a level, smooth route around the rim of the cliffs above the confluence of the Mellte and Hepste rivers.

4 From post 35, a short but very steep link path goes down steps to Sgwd y Eira. *Three curtains of water thunder over the rock face into the pool below. It is possible to go behind the waterfall, but notices warn of the risk of this and advise you not to linger.* Return up the steps to the main path to post 35 and turn right. Continue along the trail for ¾ mile as far as fingerpost 11, where the path to Gwaun Hepste veers right.

5 To return to Cwm Porth, go straight ahead. The path continues through woods, before passing in front of the buildings at Hendre-bolon. A very pleasant level track continues through limestone country for the next mile. When you reach the road, turn left to reach the entrance to the car park.

Waterfall Country
In the southern fringe of the Brecon Beacons National Park, a belt of limestone emerges on the surface. A series of tributaries of the River Neath mould caverns and pot holes beneath the surface and then create a sequence of falls where the water passes over harder sandstone. The rivers Nedd Fechan, Pyrddin, Mellte and Hepste conspire together to produce the greatest collection of cas-

START I P

Porth yr Ogof

Cwm Porth

S

cades in Wales and earn this region the title of 'Waterfall Country'. Walk 5 explores the Nedd Fechan from Pontneddfechan, while this outing discovers the waterfalls of the Mellte and Hepste from the caving centre of Cwm Porth. Walk 6 explores Sgwd yr Eira from the other bank.

Sgwd Isaf Clun Gwyn

Afon Mellte

G G

Hendre Bolon

G

G

To Gwaun Hepste

Sgŵd Clun-gwyn

5

2

N

0   Miles   ¼

Sgŵd Isaf Clun-gwyn

Sgŵd y Pannwr

steep path down

3

4

steep path down

Sgŵd y Eira

15

TRAINS, TRAMS & DAMS

DESCRIPTION A tour of the picturesque lower reaches of the Caerfanell valley and its peaceful sylvan subordinate, Cwm Banw. The captivating natural beauty of the woodlands and surrounding hills disguises a wealth of industrial archaeology. Tramway, railroad and reservoir all give clues to the strategic importance of this pass through the mountains.

DISTANCE & TERRAIN 5½ miles. Most of the route has an excellent hard-core surface, making it suitable for a wet day or muddy season.

START Forestry car park and picnic area between Talybont reservoir and Aber Village: SO 106210. Aber village is situated 2 miles south of Tal-y-bont on the minor road that traverses the mountains towards Merthyr. There is a small roadside parking area if the official car park is closed.

1 Walk north along the road, following a footpath sign, 'To the Hill'. Watch for traffic. In about 200 yards, turn left up a lane with another sign, 'To the Hill.' This refers to Waun Rydd, which rises above the forest to the west. But we're not bound for this apparently definitive elevation. Just 200 yards up the lane, leave the route to 'The Hill'. Where the lane bends to the left, cross a stile in the right hand fence and continue across the field, heading towards an old chapel. Although the OS map indicates a path below the chapel, there is no access out of the field here. Instead, a kissing gate leads into the graveyard and a path leads through this on to the lane beyond. Turn left up the lane. This climbs steadily into the hidden wooded recess of Cwm Banw. *Depending on the time of year, enjoy the festival of colour in the hedgerow. Bluebells, stichwort, herb robert, cow parsley, garlic mustard and red campion are among the plants that thrive in this habitat.* Higher up pass a house and barn. Although the lane is tarmac and open to traffic you are unlikely to encounter motor vehicles; it leads to just one house. *A variety of trees provide a sylvan home for bird life. Oak, ash, rowan, silver birch and hawthorn cling to the slope, hiding the stream down below you to the right.* A gate leads to more open country. A new section of lane diverts above a landslip. *Now you have views ahead of the high ridge from Waun Rydd. Eventually the lane ends at Nantllanerch Farm. The homestead sits snugly in the side of the cwm. The noise of a generator indicates self-sufficiency from the national grid.*

2 At the end of the lane, a series of gates leads on to a green track. This is a bridleway and is also a signed mountain bike route. Follow the track down to a ford over a small stream, just above a waterfall. Hug the fence and curve round to the right. After another gate, drop down a shady avenue between two ditches. At the bottom, cross a footbridge over the rocky fast flowing Clydach. The track then climbs up to the right. *There are good views back across Cwm Banw; pause to look at the high ridge of Ffordd Las and Waun Rydd behind you.* After a while, the lane gains a surface and continues through pine forest. *As you emerge from the trees, there are views of Tal-y-bont reservoir and east to the Black Mountains.*

3 Turn right over a stile, following a sign for Aber. You have now joined the Usk Valley Walk. Follow the left hand side of the field above the house at Pwll-y-hwyaid and find a stile under a tree just to the left of a gate. Cross the next field to another stile and descend the subsequent field diagonally. At the bottom, a post indicates the way to a short section of green lane leading to the road.

4 Turn right along the road, watching for traffic. In about 300 yards, opposite Aber Farm, turn left through a gate, still following the Usk Valley Walk. Follow the left hand side of the field, through another gate and on to a footbridge. At the far side, ignore the path to the right and continue straight ahead, across a grassy strip, and then up through a patch of woodland. At the top of some steps, pass through a gate and then

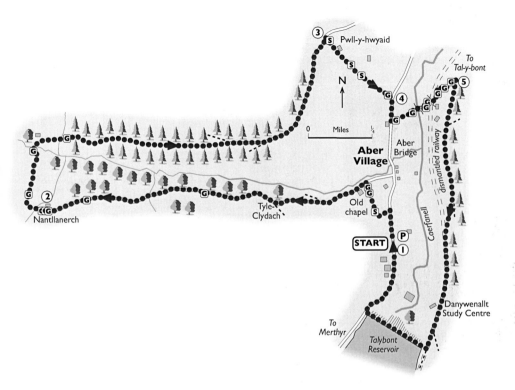

under a bridge. This carries the track of the Brecon and Merthyr Junction Railway. After the bridge, the track bears left and passes through a couple of gates. Soon after the second gate, it becomes a path and turns right to follow the edge of the field to a gate at the top. This leads to the Brinore Tramway and the Taff Trail.

5 Turn right to follow the line of the old tramroad. At an intersection of tracks, bear right and descend gently, leaving the tramway to ascend through the woods. After a while join the track bed of the Brecon and Merthyr Junction Railway and follow this to Tal-y-bont reservoir. Turn right to cross the dam wall. At the end of the dam, turn right and follow the road carefully back to the start.

Brinore Tramroad

The Tramroad opened in 1815, the year of the Battle of Waterloo. It was built to carry limestone from the quarries at Trefil, and coal from mines near Tredegar. The minerals were carried across the mountains to the canal wharf at Tal-y-bont. Horses pulled the trams up hill, while they freewheeled back down, using a wooden wedge to jam the wheels if gravity proved too generous. The tramway declined with the rise of the railways in the second half of the nineteenth century.

Tal-y-bont Reservoir

This was built to quench Newport's thirst in the 1930s. More recently, Talybont-on-Usk Energy, a community group, took over the disused turbine house to generate hydro electricity, which is sold to the national grid.

WALK 9

LLANGYNIDR, TOR Y FOEL & THE CANAL

DESCRIPTION An excellent variety of Beacons scenery. A taste of the uplands through climbing the grassy 551m pyramid of Tor y Foel, but the climb is not as long or strenuous as the highest peaks. The summit is a good viewpoint over the Usk and Caerfanell valleys. The return route descends through fields to the Brecon and Monmouthshire Canal. This gives a gentle and pleasant walk back to Llangynidr.

DISTANCE & TERRAIN 7½ miles. Field paths, with a sustained but straightforward ascent to Tor y Foel.

START Car park, opposite Llangynidr village hall. SO 156196. Llangynidr lies on the southern side of the river Usk between Crickhowell and Brecon. The B4558 runs through the village. The direct road from Llangynidr to the A40 at Bwlch crosses the river on a very narrow bridge, only suitable for ordinary cars. Otherwise, access the village via Crickhowell or Tal-y-bont. The car park is on the B4558 on the eastern side of Llangynidr. There are toilets opposite. Bus 43 runs from Abergavenny to Brecon via Llangynidr village.

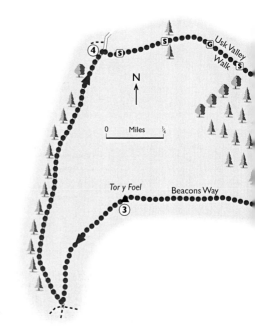

1 Walk west towards the main village for a few yards. Just opposite an old chapel, now a cycle manufacturer, turn right across a stile. Walk down the left hand side of the field. At the end, take a few steps left to find another stile. Cross this and continue across the fields to the canal. Cross the bridge, then take a half turn to the left to cross a stile, then a further half turn to the left to bring you to the towpath, where you turn right. *A lovely tree lined stretch offers views across to Bwlch on the other side of the Usk valley.* The canal bypasses the village and arrives at the Lower Lock at the bottom of the Llangynidr flight. The Coach and Horses lies just to the left, but perhaps it's too soon for refreshment! Just after a winding hole (turning point where the canal widens,

pronounced as in the 'wind' that blows) you come to Depot Lock (No 65).

2 Cross the canal using the footpath just in front of the lock. Follow the signpost with the Beacons Way logo, passing through beech and oak woods, with the Afon Crawnon tumbling down to your right. Emerging from the woods, you can see the goal, Tor y Foel, rising up to the right. Follow the waymarks up the fields, crossing a number of stiles and a farm access road. At the top of the fields, the path comes out on to an access road by a couple of houses at Pen-y-beili. At the end of this access road, go straight across the road and continue up a bridleway opposite. After a while this green lane comes up to open hillside. Keep climbing steadily and inexorably towards the top, being prepared for a few false summits! Although steep in places, the way is grassy and springy underfoot and there are excellent views on both sides of the long ridge.

3 *At 551 metres, Tor y Foel is by no means the highest ground in the area. But, because it stands alone, there are great all-round views. The ground drops away beyond*

18

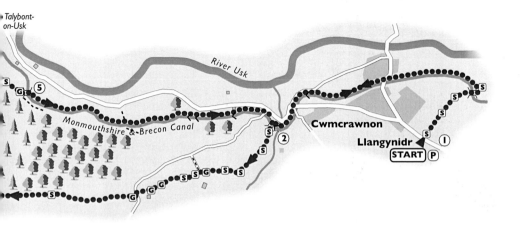

the summit into the Caerfanell valley and Tal-y-bont reservoir. From the summit bear left to continue on the broad and obvious track south westwards. It descends to the end of a tarmac road. Turn sharp right to follow this very quiet mountain road with a lovely panorama of Tal-y-bont reservoir and the forest below you.

4 After about a mile, and just before a cattle grid, turn right at a footpath sign. This is now the Usk Valley Walk. Follow the track as it curves round to a gate and a stile (don't follow another track up hill). Continue on the path as it gradually descends a field, passes through a small strip of conifers and goes across another field. Find a gate in the bottom left hand corner. Continue to follow the way markers across the fields and through a patch of woodland until you reach the canal.

5 Cross the canal and go down the steps to join the towpath. Follow this eastward and enjoy the wild flowers and trees. You pass the Llangynidr flight of locks and after a while, rejoin the outward route at lock 65. Continue back on your outward route, or if you prefer, leave the canal to walk through the village.

Monmouthshire & Brecon Canal

The navigation opened in 1812, connecting Brecon with Newport. It played a key role in the transport of minerals from the Monmouthshire iron and coalfields to the greatest port in the world. Stone from the great quarries of Llangattock and Trefil was brought by tramway to the canal and transported onwards by barge. By the 1930s the cut had fallen into disuse. But in 1970 British Waterways Board reopened parts and a 32-mile stretch from Brecon to Pontypool is now accessible for pleasant navigation on the northern fringe of the Beacons.

River Usk

The river rises south west of Sennybridge and travels through Brecon, Abergavenny and Usk to meet the Severn estuary at Newport. Its lower reaches are very deep and also have a very high tidal range, up to 30 feet. These features enabled the growth of Newport as one of the world's major ports in the nineteenth century. Its upper reaches, west of Brecon, form a key route from western Wales into England and its fertile valley forms some of the richest farming land in the country. A narrow sixteenth century bridge spans the river near Llangynidr, still open to light traffic.

AROUND & ABOUT PONTSTICILL RESERVOIR

DESCRIPTION There is a range of scenery on this 6-mile circuit of Pontsticill reservoir, the largest of four reservoirs in the Taf Fechan valley. The first section climbs moorland on the forest edge. Beyond Pontsticill, the walk makes use of the Taff Trail as it weaves its way through mixed woodland en route for Brecon. Views of the reservoir dominate much of the journey and there is an eye-catching panorama of Pen y Fan rising on the northern skyline above the Taf Fechan Forest. You also make the close acquaintance of the Brecon Mountain Railway.

DISTANCE & TERRAIN 6 miles. The first part of the route involves a climb around the moorland edge. The return is an easy stroll on forest paths and tracks.

START Car park near Dolygaer, at the head of the reservoir. SO 144054. To reach here, leave the A470 or A465 at Cefn-coed-y-cymmer, just north of Merthyr. Follow signs to Pontsticill and continue through the village towards Tal-y-bont. Pass along the west side of Pontsticill Reservoir. Just before the end, where the road turns left, continue ahead on a cul-de-sac. The car park is just on the left. You can also approach from Tal-y-bont in the north. Bus 24 (Merthyr-Pontsticill) goes close to point 5.

1 Turn left out of the car park and follow the road as it crosses the bridge between Pontsticill and Pentwyn reservoirs with fine views both ways. Continue along the road until it comes to a railway bridge. Just before the road goes underneath this, turn right to follow a path descending steeply down to the lakeshore. After a brief encounter with the water's edge, it climbs back up through the woods to run alongside the track of the Brecon Mountain Railway. *Steam trains run between Pant station and this point, before*
returning to Pontsticill station on the return journey. The path widens into a track just above the sailing club.

2 Just past the club you come to a yellow-topped post, opposite a bridge under the railway. Turn left under the bridge following a bridleway sign. At this point the main track continues level along the side of the reservoir to Pontsticill station. It is not an official right of way but seems to be used with constant impunity by tourists and locals alike as a convenient stroll and dog walk, as well as being vehicular access to the sailing club. However, our official route follows a bridleway up the hill. *It has the advantage of spectacular views across the reservoir, climbing steeply and diagonally up the hillside through forest.* At the top of the woods, go through a gate giving access to the open moorland. The bridleway now becomes indistinct and irrelevant. The next section sounds complicated, but it is less so on the ground. The key is the forest on your right, as you are effectively skirting this using the open access moorland above it. Follow the edge of the plantation, about 100 yards above its edge. A faint path appears but soon disappears in a brief squelchy marsh. Maintain the direction, with the forest edge as your guide, until you come to a small ravine just above a confluence of two streams. Climb carefully down the rather loose sheep path to the stream and continue along a narrow track on the other side. This brings you to a bridge made from an old railway sleeper that crosses the second stream.

3 Continue in the direction indicated by the plank, climbing gently up the slope in the direction of some fence posts on the horizon. If this sounds rather complicated, it is less so on the ground. *Great views open out. You have just crossed a geological boundary and have swapped the water-retaining sandstone land for porous limestone. It's much easier going and well drained. Be careful not to follow the fence as it drops precipitously down the edge of a disused limestone quarry!* Gingerly tread round the top of the unguarded cliff and notice the pitons used for rock climbing. You pick up a faint path a

5 At the top, TURN RIGHT ('The Red Cow' and the bus stop for Merthyr are just to the left.) Follow the road, with signposts to Tal-y-Bont, through the village and past the new treatment works. Just past the sign for Pontsticill reservoir, cross a stream. Leave the road here, turning left along a forest track with a sign for the Taff Trail. This rises gently into the forest, later narrowing to become a tarmac footpath. Cross a ravine on a wooden footbridge. *This is a lovely spot on the edge of the forest, with a convenient seat.* At a junction of paths, Bear left, keeping on the Taff Trail. Where it returns to the road, turn left. Soon keep straight on at a junction to follow the 'no through road' back to the car park.

little way from the edge of the escarpment. Just after a wood on your right, you come to a metal gate with a blue-topped lever. There is also a wooden post a few yards above. This gate marks re-entry to enclosed land.

4 Turn right through the gate and follow the regained bridleway as it descends diagonally above the reservoir dam, with the brooding heights of the Beacons presiding over the northern horizon. Pass under the Brecon Mountain Railway, across an access track, and on down the lane to the road at the bottom. Go through the gate into the road. Turn left and then immediately right, passing Pontsticill Water Treatment, admiring the vaguely ecclesiastical architecture of the ex-municipal utility. Cross the river and follow the side road as it twists up the hill on the opposite side.

Brecon Mountain Railway

Steam trains operate from Easter to November, with some additional Christmas specials at the end of the year. The preserved railway has operated since 1980. For much of the way, including this section, it runs along the course of the Brecon and Merthyr Railway. The first train ran on 8th August 1868 and over the years the railway brought many visitors from the industrial valleys into the Beacons and carried farmers' products from the hills to the towns. In 1873, the local Rector counted 21 trains in one day – he must have had a busy life! The line closed in 1964. The current reopened route runs from Pant station, above Merthyr, past limestone quarries and along the length of Pontsticill reservoir to a halt close to Torpantau.

21

WALK 11

AROUND THE HEAD OF THE CAERFANELL

DESCRIPTION The magnificent diversity of this walk is matched by its challenge. The approach to the hills is up a wooded ravine, where the Caerfanell drops through a series of sylvan cascades and torrents. Above this gulley, you reach the secluded cwm of Blaen-y-glyn, a wide upland amphitheatre below the high plateau of the Beacons. A pathless ascent alongside the stream brings you on to the rim of the plateau, with panoramic views on all sides. An easy but exhilarating path skirts the edge of the precipice before descending to the top of the pass at Torpantau.

DISTANCE & TERRAIN 5½ miles. An engaging expedition through rough country, pathless in places, returning along a high level cliff edge path. Take outdoor precautions and navigational equipment; probably best avoided in mist.

START Start from the car park at Pont Blaen-y-glyn, about 6 miles from Talybont on the mountain road to Merthyr. The bridge is at the bottom of the steep climb over the pass at Torpantau, and the car park is next to the stream on the north side of the road. SO 064171. Note that there are two car parks at Blaen-y-glyn. The upper car park is just under a mile away from the start at point 4 on the map..

1 Go out of the car park entrance. Turn left and cross the bridge over the stream. Immediately on the far side of the bridge, cross a stile on the left and follow the right hand bank of the stream, uphill, for about ½ mile. An attractive waterside path passes a series of tumbling falls before coming near a wooden footbridge. Don't cross this. Instead, pass a small fingerpost pointing the direction of the route which climbs steeply uphill on the right hand bank of the stream.

2 This faint, but clear, path clambers up the side; it's a bit rough in places, but clear

enough. *Enjoy the varied woodland which covers the stream's course as it plunges down a series of falls.* In about ½ mile, a stile opens the way onto unenclosed land above the tree line. Continue to climb for a while longer until arriving into an open amphitheatre of rough grassland, encircled by the lofty ridges of the Beacons plateau. The route continues on the right hand side of the stream but the path soon becomes intermittent or non-existent. Pick an appropriate course, with the main stream as your guide, heading for the nick in the skyline at the very head of the amphitheatre. Keep to the right hand side of this stream and avoid the watercourses branching right and left. In the last section, as the valley narrows, you may find it easier to cross the infant stream and trudge up its left hand bank to the plateau. Approaching the top, ignore a footpath crossing and continue for a further 200 yards to a broad junction of paths on the very brow of the ridge. *Here, for the first time, admire a view of the sandstone caps of the Beacons to the left and the Usk Valley down in front.*

3 A broad footpath traces the rim of the ridge to right and left. Don't take either of these routes. Instead, turn sharp left to follow a wide path clinging to the eastern edge of the plateau along Graig Fan Las. As you walk along the brink of the escarpment on a wonderfully airy and level path, peer down over the route you've taken through the rough bowl of Blaen-y-glyn. After a mile, the path diverts round the rocky gulley at the top of Blaen Caerfanell. The Beacons Way joins at this point and a good gravelled path continues straight ahead, still on the rim of the plateau. In ½ mile, after crossing Craig y Fan Ddu, the path drops steeply down from the heights, next to a ravine with small, but spectacular waterfalls. Reach the access road to the upper Blaen-y-glyn car park.

4 Turn left to cross a cattle grid with a kissing gate, then immediately leave the access road to take a track turning right. This weaves down through the conifer forest. Later, at a T-junction, bend to the right and continue to follow the track downhill to the lower Blaen-y-glyn car park.

Brecon & Merthyr Junction Railway

In 1858, an Act of Parliament allowed the construction of the Brecon and Merthyr Junction Railway. It eventually ran a network of lines between Newport and Brecon, providing a link between one of the world's foremost ports and mid Wales. Between Pant and Tal-y-bont, it passed through the mountains and included the 666-yard long Torpantau tunnel. The main section was closed to passenger traffic in 1962, but the route through the Beacons now forms part of the Taff Trail, a 58-mile cycling and walking route from Brecon to Cardiff. Part of the track has been reopened as the Brecon Mountain Railway.

To Fan y Big

③

Graig Fan Las

intermittent path

Blaen Caerfanell

Beacons Way

Beacons Way

Craig y Fan Ddu

faint path

Caerfanell

Falls on the Caerfanell

N

0   Miles   ¼

Waterfall

Blaen y glyn

④   grid   P

Waterfalls

Waterfalls

②

Pont Blaen-y-glyn

①   S

P   START

DESCRIPTION These two contrasting routes explore the area around Torpantau, the highest point on the road between the Usk and Taff valleys, carving a pass through the centre of the high Beacons.

WALK 12 (2 miles) is a short walk exploring the woods and cascades just above Pont Blaen-y-glyn. It follows footpaths between the lower and upper car parks, but there are plenty of variations if you want to explore other routes.

WALK 13 (8 miles) is a long and high level mountain expedition, culminating in the striking peak of Fan-y-Big. You will need a good map, compass and appropriate clothing to tackle this.

START

Upper car park at Blaen-y-glyn. SO 056175. To reach this take the mountain road between Talybont and Merthyr. The car park is about 7 miles from Talybont, at the top of the steep climb.

right and follow the path as it accompanies the stream downhill. It is a relaxed and pleasant waterside path alongside a sequence of torrents and cascades. Butterflies, such as the Orange Tip, flit across the path as they feed on vegetation along the banks. Continue until you reach the road. Cross the stile and then turn right over the bridge and the entrance to the lower car park.

3 From the far side of the car park, take a clear track which climbs steadily uphill through a blend of coniferous and deciduous woodland. After about ¼ of a mile, the track bends to the right and soon afterwards reaches the junction at Point 2. Continue straight ahead on the main path, retracing the outward route. In a little while, the path bends to the left away from the stream and ascends through the coniferous forest. In about ½ mile emerge from the trees to reach the upper car park at Blaen-y-glyn.

WALK 12
THE WOODS & WATERFALLS OF BLAEN-Y-GLYN

1 From the car park take the track going downhill from next to the cattle grid. This weaves down through the conifer forest. Later, at a T-junction, bend to the right and soon afterwards watch out for a junction leading to a footbridge across the river.

2 Turn left here, leaving the track and going through a kissing gate and over a wooden footbridge. *From the bridge, enjoy the view upstream to the spectacular waterfall.* On the far side, if you want to explore the upper falls, you can take a steep and narrow footpath marked by a wooden fingerpost. Climb this as far as you like, though it is rough in places and care is needed. Otherwise, turn

WALK 13
TORPANTAU & FAN Y BIG

1 From the car park, cross the cattle grid. Turn right up a stepped path to the left of the fence, climbing steeply through the wooded ravine of Nant Bwrefwr, beside the impressive upper waterfalls. Leaving the woodland behind, continue steeply up the moorland flank of Craig-y-Fan Ddu. After about ½ mile, gain the ridge. For nearly two miles the path hugs the edge of the plateau, with a precipitous escarpment to the right, veering around the rocky gulley of Blaen Caerfanell on the way.

Pont Blaen-y-glyn

2 *At the* end of the plateau the whole of the Usk Valley and Cwm Oergwm opens out ahead, with views of the highest Beacons away to the left. At the junction of paths, turn sharp left, and follow the rim of Cwm Oergwm for the next 1¾ miles. At first a gentle grassy slope leads to the highest point of the walk at Bwlch y Ddwyallt (754m), though there is no great topographical fanfare for the ignominious elevation. Soon afterwards the edge makes a sudden 90 degree left turn to the south west. After another ½ mile it begins to curve round back to the north west. Stone setts lead down to the col at Craig Cwmoergwm and some slate spoil adorns the route. Soon afterwards, the direct path to 'the Gap' bears left and is a short cut in poor weather or restricted time. But to conquer the summit of Fan y Big, keep ahead.

3 *Fan y Big's status as a major peak is clear at the head of the rocky spur you have just climbed. To the left the highest peaks of the Beacons range westwards. But be alert to the precipitous drop to the northwest. The route now lies left, or WSW. A steep descent*

brings you to the pass at Bwlch ar y Fan (or 'The Gap') in about ¼ mile.

4 Turn left to follow the course of the Roman road southwards through a gate and continue descending gently towards the Neuadd reservoirs. As you approach the lower reservoir, the main track turns right to the filter house and reservoir dam. Ignore this and keep straight ahead. The stony path makes a short but sharp dip to cross a gulley carrying a small stream. On the opposite side, pass through a gate and continue along a good stony track on the far side. In about ½ mile, this sidles up the tarmac road coming directly from the Lower Neuadd.

5 You touch the road but then immediately leave it to bear left, talking the Taff Trail along a level fenced track curving round the hillside for

around ½ mile until it comes to the Merthyr-Talybont road, close to its highest point at Torpantau. Turn left and follow the road for ½ mile back to Blaen y Glyn upper car park.

Bwlch ar y Fan ④

Fan y Big ③

N

0 Miles ½

Bwlch y Ddwyallt ②

Craig Cwmoergwm

Blaen Caerfanell

Beacons Way

Nant Bwrefwr

P ①

START

G ⑤

Taf Fechan Forest

Mountain Railway

WALK 14

LLANGATWG QUARRIES & CRAIG Y CILAU

DESCRIPTION Climbing from the Usk to the dramatic limestone cliffs of Mynydd Llangatwg, this 6-mile walk provides a great variety of scenery from wooded towpath to limestone heath. It explores the impressive National Nature Reserve at Craig y Cilau and offers great views across the Usk valley.

START Car park, near the parish church in Llangattock village. SO 210178. Llangattock lies on the southern bank of the Usk, opposite Crickhowell. The village can be reached from Crickhowell across the town's historic bridge, which is guarded by a set of very slow three-way traffic lights. Alternatively, you can get to Llangattock from Gilwern by the A4077. The village's car park is convenient but not well signposted. Using the tower as a landmark, find the parish church. The car park is behind a wall opposite the church. However, to reach it by car you have to continue on left past the church until a 'P' sign points through a small housing estate. Bus 43 (Abergavenny-Brecon).

I Leave the car park through the gap in the wall opposite the church. Just to your left is a water trough set in the wall. *A plaque indicates it was installed at the expense of GFW Miles Esq of Llangattock Park in 1881, alongside a quote from St John's Gospel enticing you to consider the preferable value of spiritual refreshment.* However, you need to turn right out of the car park and follow the lane back to the village's main street. Turn right here and climb gently up until you reach the Bethesda chapel on your right. Then bear right, following the sign towards Beaufort. At the end of the houses come to a bridge over the canal. Instead of crossing this, pass through the gap on to the towpath next to a small wharf. Turn left and follow the Monmouthshire & Brecon Canal. *In spring the ground is carpeted by wild flowers such as celandine and violets. The canopy*

of trees echoes to bird song. The cut follows a course a little above the valley floor, so offering glimpses through the trees across Crickhowell to the Black Mountains.

2 Leave the canal immediately before the third bridge (Pont y Parc). Cross the stile to the left and then cross the bridge to another stile on the far side. Turn left, following the opposite bank of the canal for a few yards to a third stile. Follow the direction of the yellow way marker through a small copse and diagonally across the field beyond, aiming for a barn in the top corner. A stile just to the right of the barn gives access to another field. Follow the left hand side of this for a few yards until a finger-post marks the point where you can join a tarmac lane via a stile. Turn right and follow the lane gently up hill. It soon curves right past Wenllan Farm. At a second right hand bend, turn left, forsaking the lane for a signed 'no through road'. A short stretch of tarmac leads past Ty Mawr. Pass through a gate to the left on to a green lane. *There are good views ahead to the Sugar Loaf and across the Usk Valley to the distinctly shaped Table Mountain above Crickhowell.* But you'll have more time to enjoy these later as the lane soon swings right and climbs up the slope. It becomes stonier and can be watery in wet weather. *Coppiced hedges are adorned with wild flowers such as foxgloves and Herb-Robert.* Pass a disused chapel on the left at Laswern-Isaf, now a protected site for roosting bats. *The Vincent Wildlife Trust, based in nearby Herefordshire, has established 50 reserves for bats in Wales, England and Ireland.* Just above, some fallen trees have seriously blocked the path, though you can easily avoid these by carefully following the stones around to the right. At the top, the lane turns right and levels out. Pass the house at Laswern Fawr and emerge through a gate on to a tarmac track on open mountainside. This track soon leads to a lane.

3 Turn sharp left and follow the lane a short way until it reaches the entrance to a car park (SO 209154). Follow the access road, right. When it comes to the car park

Agen Allwe

26

itself, continue ahead past a barrier on to a grassy track climbing gently towards the disused quarries. *The quarries developed because of the canal's construction. Today they are popular with rock climbers and also hide the entrance to an extensive cave system.* A few yards below a ruined kiln, bear right at a junction and follow the track as it contours below the old spoil heaps. After a while the wide track disappears at an area of huge shattered boulders, but a small path weaves its way, slanting down to join a broad pathway a little way below. When you come to this, follow it to the left, soon entering the nature reserve

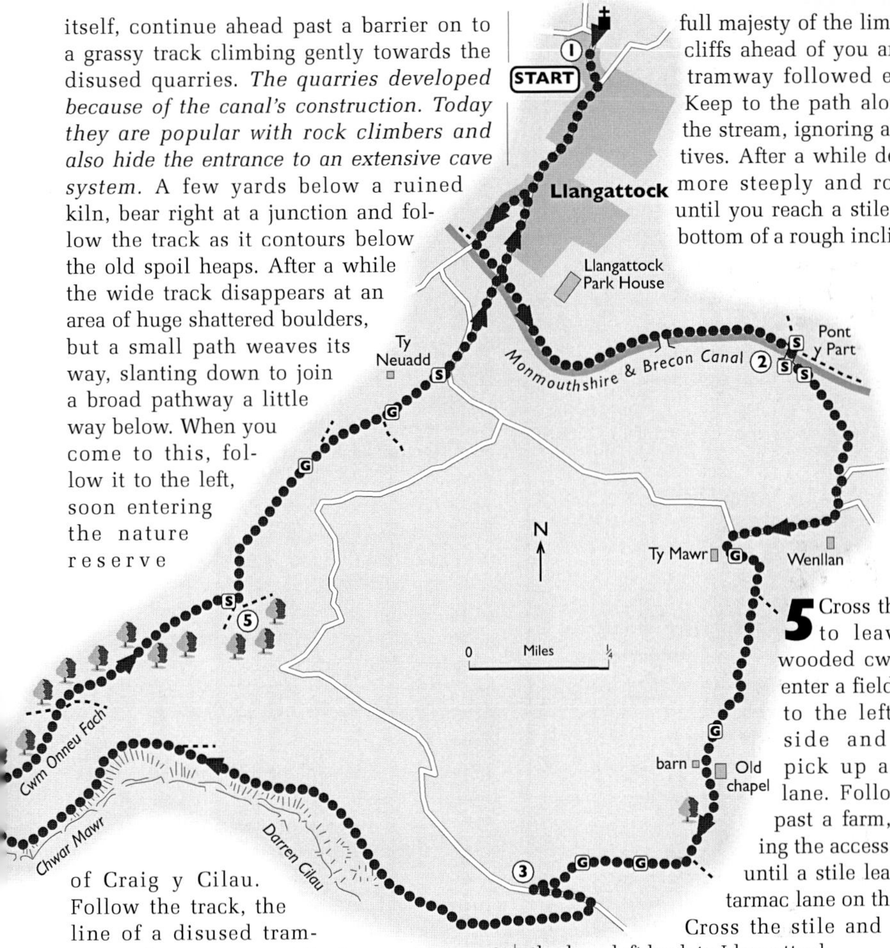

full majesty of the limestone cliffs ahead of you and the tramway followed earlier. Keep to the path alongside the stream, ignoring alternatives. After a while descend more steeply and roughly until you reach a stile at the bottom of a rough incline.

5 Cross the stile to leave the wooded cwm and enter a field. Keep to the left hand side and soon pick up a green lane. Follow this past a farm, ignoring the access tracks, until a stile leads to a tarmac lane on the right. Cross the stile and follow the lane left back to Llangattock.

Craig y Cilau National Nature Reserve

The 400 feet high cliffs and screes at Mynydd Llangatwg are one of the most dramatic manifestations of the limestone belt that marks the southern fringe of the national park. In the eighteenth and nineteenth centuries the rock was quarried and carried by incline down to the wharf at Llangattock or across the mountain by horse drawn tramway to the iron works at Brynmawr. Today the nature reserve cares for woodland and limestone habitats, home to many flowers, birds and trees, notable the rare whitebeam tree. Beneath the ground, an extensive cave system also supports a colony of lesser horseshoe bats.

of Craig y Cilau. Follow the track, the line of a disused tramway, as it curves around the inner recesses of the cwm. The residual track offers an almost effortless progress around the mountainside, with dramatic panoramas and intimate views of the cliffs above.

4 Watch out for a small yellow marker post on the right. This is the cue to leave the tramway and slant down to the right, following a smaller path. At another junction, stick with the yellow marker and descend more steeply until you reach a wall at the bottom. Turn sharp right and follow the path through the bracken at the bottom of the valley with a small stream on your left. Ignore the public footpath sign crossing the stream and climbing into the woods. Now you can see the

Map labels: START, Llangattock, Llangattock Park House, Ty Neuadd, Monmouthshire & Brecon Canal, Pont y Part, Ty Mawr, Wenllan, barn, Old chapel, Cwm Onneu Fach, Chwar Mawr, Darren Cilau, N, 0 Miles ¼

A CIRCUIT OF CWM OERGWM

DESCRIPTION An excellent route to the highest ground of the Beacons. The lower slopes provide an idyllic and intimate approach to the mountains. A waterside path with mature trees frames the distinctive sandstone caps of the Beacons. The climb up to the ridge is long but well graded. Once the height is gained, you have a day of airy and straightforward ridge walking with great all-round views.

START Llanfrynach village. SO 075257. There is no car park, but it is easy to park sensibly on the roadside in the village. Llanfrynach is three miles south east of Brecon, just off the A40 to Abergavenny. Leave the A40 half a mile east of the end of the Brecon by-pass. Turn south down the B4538 towards Tal-y-bont, immediately crossing the canal and Usk. A quarter of a mile further, turn off south to follow a minor road to Llanfrynach village. Bus 43 (Brecon-Abergavenny)

DISTANCE AND TERRAIN 10 miles. This is a long expedition and much of it is at exposed, high altitude. So take careful mountain precautions and avoid it in poor visibility.

I Next to the village hall, turn along the side road, signed to 'Cantref'. Just past Tyfry farm, the lane bears to the right. At this point, go through a kissing gate ahead and join a bridleway. Pass through a field of mature trees with the imposing house of Maesderwen to the right and the Nant Menasgin to your left. The track is obvious and the gentle pastoral scene is a delightful start to a walk with wilder pleasures in store. When the bridleway parts company with the stream, follow the way marks gently up hill to Tynllwyn farm. Passing the farm, take the path through the gate signed to 'the Hill'. Keep to the right hand side of the next field. *The first objective, Cefn Cyff ridge, rises up ahead, while the higher ground of the Beacons looms beyond.* Maintain your direction, crossing a small lane and then emerging on to a narrow road. Turn left and

follow this between hedges past a couple of houses until the tarmac ends. Turn right, following the stony track signed to Fan y Big. A short way further on a gate gives access to the open hillside.

2 A clear path climbs quite steeply up the ridge, but offers good views across the valleys on either side. After a steady ascent, the ridge levels out. *This is skylark country. Its continuous shrill song haunts the air of these hills. The notched summit of Fan y Big comes into view, while to the right the steep ridge of Bryn Teg leads to the summit of Cribyn. A glance at its merciless gradient makes you grateful that particular route has unaccountably been omitted from this book. Beyond the summit of Cribyn, the sloping plateau of Pen y Fan crowns the highest ground in the Beacons.* As the ridge steepens once again, enjoy close views of the head of the cwm, with the Roman road crossing the 'Gap', the high pass of Bwlch ar y Fan. A narrower, more airy stretch leads directly to the summit of Fan y Big.

3 *It is immediately evident that Fan y Big's status as a major peak is due to its position at the head of the rocky spur you have just climbed.* Beyond it the ground climbs gently round the summit ridge. But take care! There is a precipitous drop to the north-west. The route now lies straight ahead, almost exactly due south. Take a bearing in mist (180°). The path is clear and a stone windbreak soon confirms your course is correct. The track continues on the edge of the summit ridge with very gentle gradients. *To the right views open out across the Neuadd reservoirs with the headwaters of the Taf Fechan.* Some slate spoil marks the col at Craig Cwmoergwm and the direct path from 'the Gap' joins from the right. Bear left to join the stone setts climbing the next section. At the top, the path veers left to take a north-north easterly course, still hugging the edge of the abyss. *The successive ridges of the central Beacons range westwards, presided over by Pen y Fan, buttressed by Corn Du. Together they seem to crouch over the Usk valley like a pair of lions guarding their territory. The edge and the path suddenly turn* sharp right and you have reached the highest point of the walk at Bwlch y Ddwyallt (754m), though you would hardly notice, as there is no dramatic topographical feature to underline its significance. Keep following the path, which becomes grassier and begins to descend towards the Usk valley. In almost 2 miles, where the path forks, ignore the branch climbing up to the dome of Pen y Bryn. Instead choose the left option. This continues to drop gently through bracken until it eventually reaches a stile and gate.

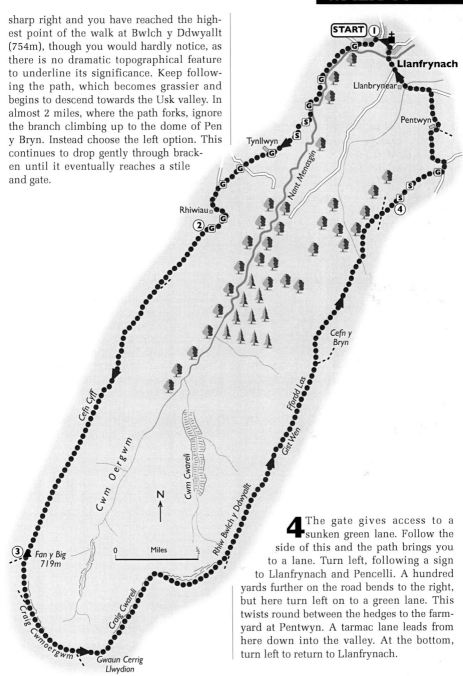

4 The gate gives access to a sunken green lane. Follow the side of this and the path brings you to a lane. Turn left, following a sign to Llanfrynach and Pencelli. A hundred yards further on the road bends to the right, but here turn left on to a green lane. This twists round between the hedges to the farmyard at Pentwyn. A tarmac lane leads from here down into the valley. At the bottom, turn left to return to Llanfrynach.

WALK 16

LLYN CWM LLWCH & CORN DU

DESCRIPTION An expedition of great variety, with a range of alternatives to suit the mood or the weather. A charming woodland valley leads into the heart of the mountains. The path climbs to a mysterious cwm cradled in the rocky arms of the Beacons' highest crags. From here, a steep ascent leads directly to a high ridge leading on up to Corn Du. On the way, you pass an obelisk honouring one young boy who lost his way here and paid with his life.

DISTANCE & TERRAIN The whole route is 5½ miles, though it can be shortened by finishing at Llyn Cwm Llwch, or by avoiding the final ascent to Corn Du. A pastoral and woodland start leads to a steep climb along a spectacular and exposed ridge.

START Parking area at the end of the lane to Cwm Llwch SO 006244. From Brecon, follow Ffrwdgrech Road. This road starts about ¼ mile towards the town centre from the western end of the Brecon by-pass where the A470 Cardiff road joins the A40 towards Llandovery. Ffrwdgrech Road leads southwards and you should keep on this lane for about 3 miles, ignoring side turnings to Cwmgwdi and elsewhere. The tarmac finishes at a gate. Go through this to the parking area on the grass beyond. There is no public transport near this route.

I *It's very tempting to linger. This is a wonderful spot. Close-cropped grass borders a sparkling stream. Mature trees, harbouring melodious birdsong, neatly frame the dramatic backdrop of the Beacons' northern face. Just the place for a picnic, but perhaps later. The best is yet to come.* Follow the track as it climbs gently towards the mountains, accompanied by the clear tumbling waters of the Nant Cwm Llwch. When you reach some sheep pens and a cottage, follow the waymarks around to the right of the property and climb two stiles to emerge into more open country. Ascend the grassy

bank on a clear track. The gradient gradually steepens towards another stile that gives access to the open hillside and National Trust land. At a cairn, bear left, heading into the heart of the cwm. Abruptly, Llyn Cwm Llwch appears at your feet, concealed until the last moment in a rocky amphitheatre. *The lake is a mysterious legacy of glacial erosion and lies embraced in the mighty arms of Pen y Fan and Corn Du. You may see tiny figures toiling up the great ridge of Corn Du above.*

2 There is a big sandstone rock where the track arrives at the water. *Use this to rest, enjoy the view and savour the tranquillity of the mountain scene.* A return to base from here will in itself be a great expedition. But if you are going any further you should be competent with a map and compass. From here, climb the faint path immediately behind the rock, as it mounts a small spur. It soon becomes clearer and steeper. Further up the slope it becomes stone set and then joins up with the direct path you left at the cairn before Llyn Cwm Llwch. Keep climbing, now gaining the edge of the ridge, later arriving at the Tommy Jones memorial, a small obelisk on the edge of the escarpment.

3 If you suddenly suffer from a shortage of enthusiasm or energy, or face the onset of poor weather, you can omit the ascent to Corn Du and descend from here by the return route. To continue towards the summit, keep going on the clear path beyond the memorial. This keeps near to the edge of the ridge and climbs directly to the summit of the Beacons' second in command. The spectacular views from the sandstone cap will not disappoint, though mist can cloak the wide vista from the Black Mountain to Radnor Forest.

4 Descend by the same path. At the Tommy Jones Memorial, continue along your outward route for about 150 yards only. Watch out for a smaller path appearing just a couple of yards to the left. There isn't exactly a junction and you will need to be observant, but it is clearly visible and represents the start of an alternative descent. Transfer across to it. If the weather is clear, your way is also easy to spot. Rather than dropping back towards Llyn Cwm Llwch, this narrower path follows a more level course around the edge of the escarpment. It soon descends gently around the edge, offering great views down into the cwm and further afield. Brecon lies clearly ahead, and beyond the hills of mid Wales. You may be able to hear the faint 'boom' of artillery shells echoing from the vast wilderness of Mynydd Eppynt across the Usk valley. A broader track joins from the left; this is the direct route from the Storey Arms. Continue on this as it descends the ridge of Pen Milan. As the ridge comes to its end, the route zig zags down and drops more gently through grass and gorse. The exact path is now not always easy to discern, but it doesn't matter. The open gorse clad hillside gradually tapers towards an apex where it meets enclosed land. This is the point you need to reach.

5 A stile leads on to a green lane. After about 100 yards, opposite a cottage, turn right across a stile. Follow the path across a series of further stiles to re-join the outward track near the parking area. Now, for that picnic!

The Tommy Jones Memorial

The grey stone monument is inscribed in memory of 5-year old Tommy Jones. He was walking with his father from Brecon station to his grandfather's farmhouse below the northern edge of the Beacons. By chance they met Tommy's grandfather and his 13-year-old cousin Willie a quarter of a mile from the house. Tommy and Willie were sent ahead to the house, but Tommy turned back, missed his way and somehow climbed up the Pen Milan ridge high into the mountains. His body was found nearly a month later. The inquest jurors used their fees to buy the memorial. Although over a century old it stands as a poignant reminder of tragedy.

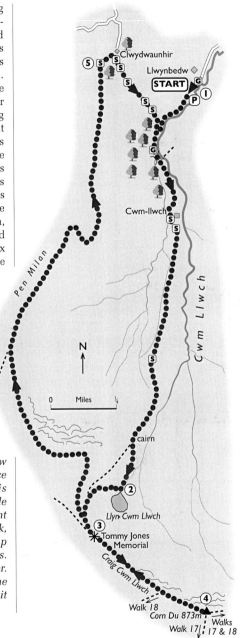

BEACONS HORSESHOE FROM THE SOUTH

DESCRIPTION A superb ridge walk around the headwaters of the Taf Fechan, with spectacular views. The circuit includes the triumvirate of Corn Du, Pen y Fan, and Cribyn.

DISTANCE & TERRAIN 6½ miles. There are two steep climbs, but most of the walk lies along the high ridges enclosing Blaen Taf Fechan. In good conditions, this is the best way to the top of the Beacons, but it is a serious mountain expedition and can be confusing in mist and potentially dangerous in poor weather.

START Lower Neuadd Reservoir. SO 032180. Larger parking areas also available at SO 037170 and at Pont Cwmyfedwen SO 043164. The Neuadd reservoirs straddle the upper reaches of the Taf Fechan, in the heart of the Brecon Beacons. To reach here, take the minor road that crosses the Beacons between Talybont-on-Usk and Merthyr. This is a spectacular traverse in itself, linking the Taf Fechan and Caerfanell valleys to carve a route through the remote spine of the mountain massif. Although it is a high-level mountain route, there is a good road. A cul de sac leads north off it at a sharp bend, close to the head of Pentwyn reservoir (SO 047157). Follow this lane for about 2 miles until the tarmac ends by the old filter house near the reservoir dam. There is no public transport near this route.

I The walk starts as near to the heart of the mountains as you could hope to be. Go through the gate at the end of the road. Follow the narrow path to the left to reach the dam wall. *The grand triumvirate of Corn Du, Pen y Fan and Cribyn stretches out across the head of the valley, while to the left, the first objective, the ridge of Graig Fan Ddu, looms above the disused reservoir. This lower reservoir has now largely drained,* but it was opened in 1884 to supply Merthyr with drinking water. Cross the dam and go through a gate to reach the open hillside. The worst is first in terms of climbing! But working on the principle that it's best to get the steep work over early in the day, you'll soon be thankful for a clockwise route. Almost immediately after the gate there is a vague bifurcation. Ignore the right hand branch that continues past a wooden pole (though it is an alternative ascent). Instead, bear left, crossing a small stream and climbing steadily and quite steeply up the slope next to a plantation. The steepest and rockiest section is towards the top, but you soon emerge suddenly on to the ridge. *Take a moment to look back across the Neuadd reservoirs. If the visibility is good, gaze across to the Sugar Loaf and Skirrid on the eastern horizon, guarding the approach from England. (See Kittiwake's book on the Black Mountains for walks on these hills near Abergavenny).*

2 Turn right and follow the path along the edge of the ridge. The way is clear and well defined. Gradients are gentle, but take care, especially in windy or slippery conditions, as the edge is precipitous. A cairn marks the alternative and rockier route up from Neuadd. Just over a mile along the ridge, another cairn just to the left of the path signals a narrower section of ridge known as Rhiw yr Ysgyfarnog. *In good weather, westward views open up across the Black Mountain of Carmarthenshire and as far as the Gower.* In mist, progress is featureless but the route is clear. Eventually the ridge curves right around the head of the Taf Fechan valley and drops slightly to the col at Bwlch Duwynt. Here is a major junction of paths.

3 The direct route from Storey Arms on the A470 joins from the left (Walk 18). A right fork provides a direct path to Pen y Fan, avoiding Corn Du. But having come so far, it seems a pity to miss the short ascent up the latter's impressive rocky cone, so CONTINUE AHEAD up the stony steps to conquer the sandstone buttress of the Beacons' second highest peak.

4 From the top of Corn Du, follow the rocky path due east (90°) from the summit. Use a compass in misty weather. The path descends a short way to the pass and then rises to the summit of Pen y Fan.

5 Leave the summit across the sloping plateau heading towards the third peak, Cribyn. In mist check your direction using a compass and a bearing of 150°. At the end of the plateau the descent becomes steep and rocky, though steps reduce the effects of erosion and ease progress. Near the bottom, the path divides. Straight ahead lies the Cribyn 'avoiding route'. This is a tempting option with the steep pyramid ahead of you and it could be useful if time is short. Otherwise, maintain resolve and bear left to follow the ridge path down to the bwlch. From here it is a steady slog up Cribyn's summit cone, though a well-made path helps. Once at the top, this route seems tame compared to the horrors of the north ridge on your left. Take care on the summit, for there are steep drops. Follow the path on a bearing of 150° and descend reasonably gently on a clear path. The gradient steepens as you approach Bwlch ar y Fan, more generally known in English as 'The Gap'. *The justification for this nomenclature and the prefixed definite article is clear. This is a key natural break in the highest ground of the Beacons. The Taf Fechan and Nant Cynwyn almost join, providing a course for the gently graded path that crosses the watershed between the southern valleys and Brecon. This is an ancient route; the site of a Roman road.*

6 Turn right to follow the course of the Roman road southwards through a gate and continue descending gently towards Neuadd reservoirs. As you approach the lower reservoir, the track is forced to turn right in front of a gulley blocked by a landslide. From here it leads directly and quickly back down to the starting point.

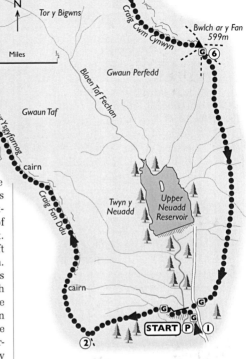

Pen y Fan

At 886m (2960 feet) this is the highest point in Britain south of Snowdonia. Much of the highest land is in the care of the National Trust; Eagle Star Insurance gifted this area to the Trust in 1965. The wide panorama confirms the topographical significance of this rocky summit. Northwards, the eye is drawn across the broad pastoral acres of the Wye Valley to the rolling hills of mid Wales. Eastwards, Llangorse Lake shimmers at the foot of the Black Mountains. To the west the vast wilderness of Fforest Fawr and the Black Mountain stretches towards the sea. Southwards lie the coal and iron valleys of South Wales reaching down to the Bristol Channel. Far below, Llyn Cwm Llwch lies in a deep glacial hollow (see Walk 16).

THE BEACONS FROM STOREY ARMS

DESCRIPTION This is the quickest and easiest way up to the two highest summits of the Brecon Beacons. It is also the most popular, so it is busy on weekends. Nevertheless, it is a satisfying and interesting ascent.

DISTANCE & TERRAIN 4½ miles. Steady ascent on good, well-made paths, making navigation relatively easy. But this is still a serious mountain expedition. The weather can be very different on the top and on a cold misty day you could be a million miles from the main north-south Wales trunk road rather than just two and a half. So take the usual precautions and make sure you carry a compass, and can use it!

START Lay-by ½ mile south of the Storey Arms, on the A470 mid way between Brecon and Merthyr. SN 987199. A substantial off-road lay-by crowns the summit of the A470 between Cardiff and Merthyr, just a few hundred yards south of the Storey Arms. There is free parking, though it gets busy on weekends and at bank holidays. There are toilets here and often a mobile catering van. Bus service Brecon – Merthyr – Cardiff.

I Walk north through the lay by and then continue on along the verge of the main road, until you reach the Storey Arms. *This was once a coaching inn on the Brecon to Merthyr road which then became a youth hostel and is now an outdoor centre owned by Cardiff Council. However, other refreshment opportunities are usually available in various lay bys on this stretch of road, offering the usual variety of fried sandwiches and drinks.* Immediately after the Storey Arms, turn right by a red phone box and follow a sign to cross a stile.

2 A well-constructed stone path climbs up from the Storey Arms. This combats erosion caused by the feet of many thousands of walkers. It also makes the going relatively

easy all the way round. Soon there are views down the Taff Fawr valley, with the three reservoirs serving Cardiff's aqueous needs. As you come to the top of a shoulder of land, the flat summit plateau of Corn Du comes into view, perched like a hat on the horizon. A short descent is now required to cross the very highest reaches of Cardiff's river at Blaen Taff Fawr.

3 Stepping-stones cross the stream and then the climb begins in earnest. It's a well graded route, with excellent views and not unreasonably steep. As you near the summit cone, the path up from Llyn Cwm Llwch merges from the left (see Walk 16). The final ascent is steeper and the path is right by the edge of the escarpment. *There's a good view down into the glacial hollow of Llyn Cwm Llwch and you can see the Tommy Jones memorial obelisk further down the ridge.* A final rocky section leads to the summit of Corn Du.

4 From the top of Corn Du, it is possible to miss out the second summit, Pen y Fan, by following the path south from the summit to Bwlch Duwynt. This may be useful if time is short, but it is just a short way on to the final goal and it would be a shame not to complete the walk if all is well. To reach Pen y Fan, take the path east (90°) from the summit. It soon descends and curves round in an east northeasterly direction, quickly reaching the bwlch between the two highest beacons. A short ascent brings you to the summit of the national park, Pen y Fan, at 886 metres.

5 *This is higher than anywhere in Wales (outside Snowdonia), or in England (outside Cumbria). So you can expect a fine view on a clear day, though you would be unwise to take this for granted! The panorama is extensive. South, over the old coal and iron valleys of South Wales and out across the Bristol Channel to the purple haze of Exmoor. The island of Steep Holme rises in the middle of the Severn Estuary. Northwards, the eye is drawn over the Usk and Wye catchments to Radnor Forest, and the Clee Hills of southern Shropshire. West*

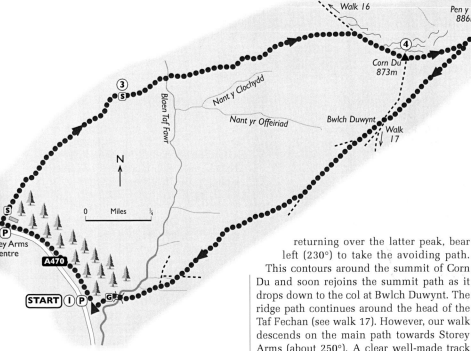

and northwest the ranks of hills and ridges of mid Wales march towards the far horizon. To the east, you can gaze across the Wye valley to the northern escarpment of the Black Mountains. Return by your outward route (about 220°) to the lowest point between Pen y Fan and Corn Du. Instead of returning over the latter peak, bear left (230°) to take the avoiding path. This contours around the summit of Corn Du and soon rejoins the summit path as it drops down to the col at Bwlch Duwynt. The ridge path continues around the head of the Taf Fechan (see walk 17). However, our walk descends on the main path towards Storey Arms (about 250°). A clear well-made track leads directly down to the main road. *Just before the bottom, pass a plaque on the right commemorating the gift of the Beacons to the National Trust by Eagle Star Insurance in 1965. A new wooden footbridge evades the stepping-stones and a gate leads through a patch of woodland back to the lay by.*

Corn Du

35

CRAIG CERRIG-GLEISIAD & FAN FRYNYCH

DESCRIPTION An adventurous circuit of a classic glacial cwm, carved by ice, colonised by Iron Age dwellers, medieval farmers and rare alpine plants. It climbs directly through the secretive cwm and along the top of a dramatic rocky escarpment.

DISTANCE & TERRAIN 3 miles. This is one of the shortest walks in the book but also one of the most demanding. It requires care and is best avoided altogether in high wind or icy conditions. There is a steep and loose descent.

START Lay-by and picnic site on northbound side of A470, SN 971223. To reach the start, take the A470 from either Brecon or Merthyr. There is a lay-by about 1½ m north of Storey Arms. Bus service (Brecon – Merthyr – Cardiff) runs along the A470.

1 Go through the kissing gate signed to Twyn Dylluan Du and Forest Lodge. Climb a well-made path up through woodlands just above a stream. At the wall, go through the gap next to the gate. Continue straight ahead towards the amphitheatre of cliffs, next to the stream. You've entered another world. *The traffic noise has abated and the main road is completely out of view.* Trees cling precariously to the precipitous rocky crags that surround the hidden bowl. Below, heather and ferns carpet the ground and a lovely grassy path takes you up into the cwm. Further up a sign asks you to bear left to avoid an eroded mound. *This is glacial moraine, capped by the site of an Iron Age settlement. This area has been used for centuries as summer pasture. There are remains of fields and house platforms from the Middle Ages when farmers lived here with their stock during the summer months.* The path circumnavigates the mound and then climbs more steeply up the escarpment. Just below the brow, a white waymark indicates a path left. Follow this as it rises gently

and arrives at a gate in the ridge fence.

2 To visit the top of Fan Frynych, turn right here and follow the broad track. It rises gently to the summit plateau with fine views across Brecon and on to the northern profile of the Black Mountains. *Pen y Fan and Corn Du dominate the eastern horizon across Glyn Tarell.* At the highest point of the ridge, you reach an area of hollows. The trig point, a white concrete pillar, lies about 200 yards to the left of the track and is reached by a small path. This could be confusing in mist so if in doubt stay on the track. On a clear day the detour is worth it for the views westwards.

3 From the summit retrace your steps to point 2, where you originally gained the ridge. Continue ahead with the fence on your left to a shallow depression with a pond. Cross over two stiles and continue ahead on the path, this time with the fence on the right. Don't wander too far from the path, as there are steep cliffs on your left. The path climbs up to the top of Craig Cerrig-gleisiad.

4 From here the path curves round the top of the precipice with good views down into the cwm. Take care here as there is no fence on the edge. The descent also requires great caution. It is steep and often slippery. You will probably need to use both hands and feet and certainly take your time. The path brings you to the bottom of the cwm at the gate. Return down the path to the car park.

Craig Cerrig-gleisiad & Fan Frynych National Nature Reserve

This spectacular reserve covers two great rocky amphitheatres created by the last ice age. You encircle Craig Cerrig-gleisiad on this walk. (Craig Cwm-du and the summit of Fan Frynych are visited on Walk 20 from the National Park Mountain Centre.) Around twenty thousand years ago a glacier carved out the 500-foot cliffs. As the climate warmed, the retreating ice left rocks behind in the hollowed-out cwms. These moraines, now covered by grass, are the humps and bumps you can see today.

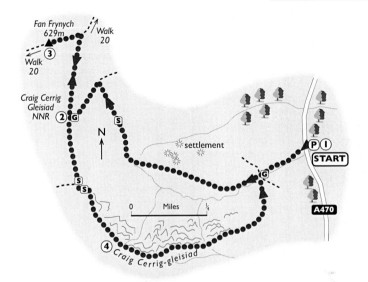

Craig Cerrig-gleisiad is north facing and reaches a height of over 600 metres above sea level. It therefore provides the southernmost British habitat for mountain plants such as purple saxifrage and mossy saxifrage. These arctic species do not occur again until the Alps. You may also see wild ponies and Welsh Black cattle.

Fan Frynych

FAN FRYNYCH & CRAIG CWM-DU

DESCRIPTION Fan Frynych dominates the view southwards from the Mountain Centre. Its shapely profile marks the northernmost ridge of Fforest Fawr, the vast area of moorland west of the upper Taf. Its most impressive features are the two north-facing precipitous crags of Craig Cerrig-gleisiad and Craig Cwm-du. The former is visited on Walk 19. Craig Cwm-du, the highlight of this walk, is a remote and isolated cwm, colonised by alpine plants and visited by the red kite. The whole area from point 2 is included in a national nature reserve.

DISTANCE & TERRAIN 6½ miles. The outward route lies over the main ridge of Fan Frynych, culminating in a descent to Craig Cwm-du. In mist this part of the walk requires careful navigation and competent use of a compass. The return is along an easy and clear track following the base of the ridge and overlooking the Usk and Senni valleys.

START Brecon Beacons National Park Mountain Centre SN 977263. The Mountain Centre is signposted along a lane from Libanus, on the A470 Brecon-Merthyr road. It is about 1½ miles from the turning. You can also reach it from the A4215 road from Sennybridge.

1 Turn left out of the Mountain Centre car park and follow the road 200 yards to a T-junction. Go straight across, following a track over the common, with a wood on the left and the bulk of Fan Frynych ahead of you. At the end of the common, you join a farm access track, which leads to a road. Go straight across the road, following a lane signposted to Forest Lodge. In just over half a mile, where the tarmac lane turns sharp right to a group of buildings, keep straight ahead along a stony track with a wood on your right. About ½ mile further, cross a cattle grid and go through a gate.

2 Turn left. A signpost a little way back from the junction indicates the route to

the A470 and Llwyn-y-celyn youth hostel. The track heads directly towards the hillside and at its base passes the entry sign to Craig Cerrig-gleisiad National Nature Reserve. The route bears left here to slant diagonally up the side of the hill. As it gains the crest of the hill, turn sharp right to stay on the main track. This now climbs steadily up the nape of the ridge. *There are good views left across Glyn Tarell, with the A470 snaking up to Storey Arms.* The flat caps of Corn Du and Pen-y-fan dominate the scene. *Take a moment to look behind and enjoy the panorama over Brecon to the Black Mountains and beyond.* As you reach the highest point of the ridge, take care to look out for the white painted trig point, set back about 200 yards to the right of the track. A path turns right off the main track to reach this, but in mist the navigation may be tricky. If you find the main track is starting to descend, you have gone too far. The OS column marks the highest point of Fan Frynych at 629 metres. *The view now extends westwards to the Black Mountain. You can also see the two great crags of Craig Cerrig-gleisiad (Walk 19) and Craig Cwm-du, peeping over the wide moorland horizon.*

3 Continue straight ahead from the summit (bearing 250°), following the broad and rather squelchy track across the grassy plateau. Gradually descend for about half a mile.

4 Watch out for a well-made stone cairn standing just a few yards to the left of the path. This is the marker for the diverging route to Craig Cwm-du. If you want to shorten the walk, the main track ahead winds on down to point 5. However, to follow the complete route, turn left (205°) on to a narrower but initially clear path past the cairn. This descends gently at first, but soon becomes much steeper; it is also less evident on the ground. However, if you maintain this direction, you will drop down to the upper reaches of Nant Cwm-du, reaching a small stream deep in the defile. Turn right and follow the stream downhill. The small path becomes broader and crosses and re-crosses the water with the aid of a couple of footbridges. *To the left, the towering crags of Craig Cwm-du stretch up to the sky, trees clinging to the vertiginous slopes.* Reaching the heart of the cwm, you realise what a very special place this is, and the chances are you will have it all to yourself.

5 The path comes to a T-junction with a wider track. Just a few yards to the left, this track follows the ancient Roman road of Sarn Helen, climbing between Fan Nedd and Fan Llia on its way to the garrison fortress at Neath. However, we turn right here. The stony track rises slightly and curves round the western flank of Fan Frynych, with pretty views across Heol Senni.

6 Continue straight ahead as a track joins from the right. This is the direct (shorter) route from Fan Frynych's summit that diverged at Point 4. The walk now continues along a shelf of rough pasture between the rising bulk of the mountain and the valley below. You rejoin the outward route at point 2, continuing back to the Mountain Centre by the outward course.

Craig Cwm-du

Craig Cwm-du is part of the National Nature Reserve covering the whole of Fan Frynych. The array of spectacular cliffs shelters an isolated and remote cwm, origin of a minor tributary of the Senni. The trees and shrubs clinging to the cliffs make this an unusual habitat and the crags are known for their Welsh poppies. About 80 species of birds have been seen in the whole reserve area, and this wild corner is a good place to see red kites and other raptors wheeling overhead.

Sensible precautions

OS Explorer maps 12 & 13 cover all the walks. Always wear walking boots and be prepared to use a compass or GPS equipment. Tell someone where you are going and stick to your route. **Never** be too proud to turn back. The mountains will be here tomorrow. *Make sure you are too.*

Appropriate public transport information is included in the introduction to each walk, where links exist. Regular buses link Brecon with Abergavenny, Merthyr and Llandovery. The nearest railway stations are Abergavenny and Merthyr.

KEY TO THE MAPS

— Main road
— Minor road
•-▶- Walk route and direction
① Walk instruction
- - - Path
∿ River/stream
Ⓖ Gate
Ⓢ Stile
△ Summit
🌲🌳 Woods
🍺 Pub
Ⓟ Parking

THE COUNTRYSIDE CODE

- Be safe – plan ahead and follow any signs
- Leave gates and property as you find them
- Protect plants and animals, and take your litter home
- Keep dogs under close control
- Consider other people

Open Access
Some routes cross areas of land where walkers have the legal right of access under The CRoW Act 2000 introduced in May 2005. Access can be subject to restrictions and closure for land management or safety reasons for up to 28 days a year. Details from: www.naturalresourceswales.gov.uk. Please respect any notices.

Published by
Kittiwake Books Limited
3 Glantwymyn Village Workshops, Glantwymyn, Machynlleth, Montgomeryshire SY20 8LY

© Text & map research: Alastair Ross 2016
© Maps & illustrations: Kittiwake 2016
Drawings by Morag Perrott

Cover photos: *Main:* Pant y Creigiau & Talybont Reservoir. *Inset:* Monmouthshire & Brecon Canal.
Photos supplied by www.alamy.com

Printed by Mixam, UK.

ISBN: **978 1 908748 36 2**